The 2024 Showdown

Inside the Race for the White House

By

Dr. David K. Ewen

ISBN: 9798871963913
Imprint: Independently published

Cover art by Samuel Branch via Unsplash

About the Book

This book offers a comprehensive and insightful analysis of the highly anticipated 2024 presidential election. With the world eagerly anticipating another defining moment in American politics, the author delves deeply into the political landscape. This exploration scrutinizes the key players, their strategies, and the potential outcomes of this consequential race.

Through meticulous research and a balanced approach, the book provides readers with a unique perspective on the candidates, their policies, and the critical issues that will mold the nation's future. It navigates the intricate dynamics of the primaries, the intensity of the campaign trail, and the pivotal factors that could influence the electorate.

From delving into historical contexts to predicting potential impacts on both domestic and international affairs, this book ensures readers gain a comprehensive understanding of the complexities and subtleties of the 2024 presidential election. Through engaging storytelling and thought-provoking analysis, the author invites readers to critically evaluate each candidate's strengths and weaknesses. This encourages a deeper appreciation for the democratic process and underscores the power of an informed electorate.

Whether you're a political enthusiast seeking in-depth knowledge or an everyday citizen aiming to make informed decisions, this book stands as an invaluable resource. It sheds light on the inner workings of one of the most significant events in American politics. By unraveling the intricacies of the 2024 presidential election, the author empowers readers to engage in meaningful discussions and take an active role in shaping the future of their country.

About the Author

Dr. David K. Ewen's formidable expertise in international affairs and his acute comprehension of the global impact of the 2024 election stem from his extensive background as an international university professor with a specialization in global communications studies. His career has uniquely equipped him with the insights and analytical tools needed to assess the multifaceted implications of political events on a global scale.

As a seasoned academic in global communications studies, Dr. Ewen possesses a nuanced understanding of how political processes, including elections, resonate beyond national borders. His scholarly pursuits have delved deeply into the interconnectedness of politics, media, and international relations, emphasizing the intricate ways in which communication shapes perceptions and influences global perspectives.

Through his research and teachings, Dr. Ewen has elucidated the intricate dynamics between political communication, media narratives, and international relations. His expertise extends to comprehending how political campaigns, rhetoric, and messaging strategies employed during elections can reverberate across diverse cultures and societies worldwide.

Given his academic prowess, Dr. Ewen is adept at dissecting the global implications of the 2024 election. He approaches this task by scrutinizing how the outcomes, policies, and geopolitical shifts resulting from the election might impact international relations, global alliances, and the communication strategies adopted by different nations.

Dr. Ewen's unique perspective is grounded in his comprehensive understanding of how information flows, technological advancements, and cultural nuances intersect within the realm of global communication. This expertise allows him to discern the broader implications of political events like the 2024 election, considering how they may influence diplomatic relations, trade dynamics, and the global perception of nations involved.

His insights are not solely theoretical; they are informed by real-world observations, scholarly research, and an acute awareness of the evolving landscape of global communication technologies and their impact on international affairs.

Dr. David K. Ewen's proficiency in global communications studies serves as an invaluable lens through which to interpret the global ramifications of significant political events like the 2024 election. His analytical acumen and deep-rooted knowledge contribute significantly to unraveling the intricate web of connections between politics, communication, and the broader international landscape.

Dr. David K. Ewen

Table of Contents

Chapter 1: Introduction to the Race

The 2024 US presidential election promises to be a captivating and historically significant event, with several key aspects worth examining. The 2024 US presidential election promises a captivating journey, filled with suspense, intrigue, and historical significance. By understanding the key drivers, timeline, and opportunities for engagement, you can navigate this momentous event and actively participate in shaping the future of your nation.

Chapter 2: The Candidates for 2024

As of January 2024, the United States is abuzz with preparations for the forthcoming presidential election, showcasing prominent candidates from both the Democratic and Republican parties. Within the Democratic realm, President Joe Biden has announced his candidacy for re-election, aiming to build upon the accomplishments and policies of his initial term. Alongside Biden, a slate of third-party contenders seeks the Democratic nomination, each bringing unique perspectives and proposals to the forefront.

On the Republican side, the field is brimming with notable figures, notably including former President Donald Trump, a polarizing yet influential figure within the party. Despite previous controversies during his tenure, Trump retains a steadfast base of support, emerging as the favored choice for about half of Republican and Republican-leaning independent registered voters seeking the party's nomination.

Joining the Republican fray are several noteworthy candidates. Florida Governor Ron DeSantis, acclaimed for his conservative policies and management of the COVID-19 pandemic in his state, stands out prominently. Former New Jersey Governor Chris Christie enters the race, leveraging his political acumen and experience. North Dakota Governor Doug Burgum, known for his innovative governance methods, adds diversity to the Republican field.

Beyond these seasoned politicians, a few unexpected entrants bring a fresh perspective to the Republican nomination contest. Philosopher Cornel West, recognized for his progressive ideals and activism, offers a distinctive angle to the race. Senator Tim Scott, a respected figure within the party, presents a conservative governing approach. Businessman and pastor Ryan Binkley, with his distinct background and values, seeks to impact the political landscape. Lastly, talk radio host Larry Elder brings his media presence and connection with conservative voters to the forefront.

While the Republican landscape boasts diversity with notable contenders, Donald Trump remains a towering figure within the party. Nevertheless, candidates such as Ron DeSantis, Nikki Haley, Vivek Ramaswamy, and Chris Christie are gaining momentum and could potentially pose a formidable challenge to Trump's bid for the Republican nomination. The unfolding election season promises intrigue as these candidates maneuver the political terrain, vying to captivate the attention and support of voters nationwide.

Chapter 3: The Rematch Potential

The prospect of a Biden-Trump rematch looms large, presenting a clash between two towering figures embodying deeply divided ideologies, poised to reshape the political landscape for years. The intensity of their rivalry and contrasting visions would undoubtedly create a fiery and captivating race. However, recent polls indicate that most Americans aren't particularly thrilled about the potential rematch. According to The Associated Press-NORC Center for Public Affairs Research, a majority of U.S. adults would feel dissatisfied with either Biden or Trump as their party's nominee in 2024. Another poll by Reuters/Ipsos depicted a closely contested hypothetical head-to-head matchup between the two, with Trump holding a slight lead. Nonetheless, there's a pervasive sense of apathy among voters, with many expressing discontents with the two-party system and yearning for an alternative choice. These findings suggest that while a Biden-Trump rematch might attract attention, it doesn't necessarily evoke enthusiasm among the American public.

The ideological disparities between Joe Biden and Donald Trump span various policy realms. On abortion rights, Biden is "pro-choice" while Trump is "pro-life." Their stances on immigration differ significantly, with Biden advocating for the DREAM Act and a pathway to citizenship for undocumented immigrants, while Trump favors deportation and a border wall. The divergence continues in areas like gun control, where Biden seeks expansion of regulations while Trump does not. Taxation also reveals stark contrasts, with Biden aiming to raise taxes on corporations and high-income earners while Trump implemented tax cuts. Additionally, their economic plans diverge, with Biden prioritizing climate change within his infrastructure focus. Moreover, their respective voter bases are notably different, with Trump drawing substantial support from white, working-class voters. These policy disparities and voter base distinctions underscore the deeply divided ideologies they represent.

The personal traits and leadership styles of Biden and Trump further contribute to their differing visions. Biden is perceived as more cooperative, favoring moderate policy tools and emphasizing rewards and promises. In contrast, Trump's leadership style leans toward aggression and confrontation, often employing extreme language and tactics in decision-making. These distinct leadership approaches shape their visions and contribute to the chasm in their ideologies.

In conclusion, the possibility of a Biden-Trump rematch evokes varied responses among the American populace. Despite the anticipation of a politically charged showdown carrying significant implications, recent polling data unveils a lack of fervor among voters. The stark disparities in their policies, the diversity within their support bases, and their distinctly contrasting leadership styles underline the profound ideological chasm they represent. Whether this rematch comes to fruition or not, the collision between these political giants has left an enduring mark on American politics, destined to influence and sculpt the national discourse for years to come.

The potential clash between Biden and Trump symbolizes more than a mere electoral contest; it signifies a deeper societal and ideological divide within the country. Their policy divergences, ranging from matters like immigration and taxation to social issues like abortion and gun control, illustrate the contrasting visions they offer to the nation.

Moreover, the distinct voter bases they appeal to further accentuate the broader rifts within American society. Trump's significant support among white, working-class voters contrasts sharply with Biden's more diverse coalition. These differences in support highlight the varied perspectives and priorities that exist across the American electorate.

Chapter 4: Who Will Win?

The upcoming 2024 presidential race stands poised on a precipice of uncertainty, hinging on a complex interplay of factors such as candidates, campaign strategies, and the ever-evolving political landscape. Recent data from a Wall Street Journal poll reflects a decline in President Biden's approval ratings, with a hypothetical matchup showing him trailing Donald Trump by a 4-percentage-point margin. However, the considerable time until the election suggests a malleable political environment prone to transformation. The forecast for the 2024 Presidential Election remains uncertain, accentuated by the unique unfavorability of both candidates, further complicating the scenario. A Morning Consult survey underscores this uncertainty by indicating a dead heat between Biden and Trump, with a notable 10% of voters supporting alternative candidates and 4% undecided, emphasizing the fluidity of the race.

Adding an intriguing dimension, political analyst Allan Lichtman, renowned for his accurate predictions, posits that Biden seeking re-election could favor the Democratic party significantly. This speculation, albeit thought-provoking, remains one among many perspectives, highlighting the multitude of factors influencing the election's trajectory.

Navigating the dynamic realm of politics renders predicting the 2024 presidential race a formidable challenge. Shifts in public opinion driven by unforeseen events, intertwined with vital factors like economic status, global relations, and domestic concerns, will wield substantial influence. Equally pivotal will be the candidates' campaign strategies, shaping voter perception and support.

The ultimate outcome of the 2024 presidential race is a product of a complex blend of elements, making it resistant to definitive prediction. The ever-evolving political landscape involves numerous factors that exert influence during an election, each capable of swaying the final result. Although current polls and analyses offer valuable insights into potential outcomes, they should not be treated as infallible indicators of what's to come. The dynamics of an election are intricate, susceptible to unforeseen events or shifts in public sentiment that can dramatically alter its course.

As the election approaches, candidates will confront a spectrum of challenges and opportunities, each contributing to shaping the narrative and influencing voters' decisions. It becomes imperative for voters to remain well-informed, critically engage with the information presented to them, and meticulously evaluate the platforms put forth by the candidates. By aligning their choices with personal values and priorities, voters can make informed decisions that resonate with their beliefs and aspirations for the future.

Chapter 5: Trump's Enduring Base

Former President Donald Trump continues to wield significant influence within the Republican Party despite exiting the office. This enduring support significantly impacts both the party's nomination process and the overall turnout in general elections. Recent findings from an NBC News poll reveal that roughly one-third of Republicans and those leaning toward the party still identify more with Trump than the broader Republican establishment. This steadfast allegiance underscores Trump's enduring sway and impact on his base.

Moreover, a survey conducted by The Bulwark and Republican pollster Whit Ayres highlighted that 28% of Republican primary voters would back Trump even if he chose to run independently. This statistic underscores the remarkable strength of Trump's personal brand and emphasizes how his supporters prioritize him over traditional party loyalties. Another poll by The Associated Press-NORC Center for Public Affairs Research unveiled that a substantial 63% of Republicans desire Trump to run for office again, with 70% maintaining a favorable opinion of him. These numbers underscore the depth and widespread nature of Trump's support within the party.

With such a robust foundation of support, Trump stands in a potent position to significantly shape the Republican nomination process. His influence could potentially mold the party's platform and even impact the selection of its candidates. Additionally, this sturdy support base could translate into a substantial voter turnout for Trump during general elections.

Despite his significant support within the Republican Party, it's important to recognize that Donald Trump's appeal may not hold the same sway among independent and swing voters. Securing backing from these demographics would be crucial for Trump to clinch victory in a general election. While Trump undeniably commands a strong following within the GOP, his broader appeal among voters beyond the party lines remains a topic of debate and could present a potential obstacle to his electoral success.

Trump's ability to resonate with independent and swing voters, who often hold the balance in national elections, is essential. These voters might not have the same allegiance to party figures and tend to assess candidates based on their policies, demeanor, and broader appeal rather than just party affiliation. For Trump to secure victory in a general election, he would need to broaden his support base beyond staunch Republican supporters and resonate with a more diverse range of voters.

While his core supporters remain fervently loyal, Trump's approach and rhetoric have been divisive, which could potentially hinder his ability to attract voters from outside his immediate base. His strategies and messaging would likely need to evolve to resonate with a wider audience and address the concerns and priorities of a more diverse electorate.

Consequently, while Trump's influence within the Republican Party is undeniable and holds immense weight during primaries and in shaping party dynamics, his ability to garner broader support from independent and swing voters is pivotal for success in a general election. The challenge lies in expanding his appeal beyond his dedicated base and resonating with a more diverse set of voters to secure a path to victory.

Chapter 6: Example Candidate Impact

Nikki Haley, the former governor of South Carolina and a former U.S. ambassador to the United Nations, has recently captured headlines by announcing her candidacy for the 2024 United States presidential election. With a prominent standing in American politics, Haley brings a substantial political background, having previously held the governorship of South Carolina and served as a U.S. ambassador, providing her with extensive experience in both domestic governance and international relations.

One notable facet of Haley's political journey is her public criticism of former President Donald Trump during his initial presidential campaign. This stance highlighted her independent thinking and readiness to hold powerful figures accountable, even within her own party. While some may question her decision to challenge Trump, it underscores her commitment to principles and her willingness to express her convictions, traits often sought by voters in a presidential candidate.

Since declaring her candidacy, Haley has swiftly gained attention and support, propelling her to the forefront of the Republican nomination race for the 2024 presidential election. Her robust political track record, coupled with her capacity to engage with constituents and tackle complex issues, has generated significant momentum for her campaign. As a woman with an immigrant background, Haley also offers a unique perspective that may resonate with diverse voter groups seeking representation and inclusivity in leadership roles.

As the 2024 presidential election approaches, Nikki Haley's candidacy emerges as a potential catalyst, poised to reshape the political landscape. Her remarkable experience, principled approach, and exceptional ability to resonate with voters position her as a compelling and influential contender. Having served as the United States Ambassador to the United Nations during the Trump administration and previously as the Governor of South Carolina, Haley brings a wealth of knowledge spanning domestic and international affairs. Her pragmatic policy-making and adept navigation of complex political terrains have solidified her reputation as a skilled and effective leader.

What sets Haley apart is her unique talent for forging personal connections with voters, transcending political divides. Whether through her speeches, interviews, or social media presence, she effectively communicates her ideas and values, captivating a diverse audience. This ability to inspire and engage individuals distinguishes her as a candidate capable of resonating with a broad spectrum of the electorate.

Regardless of whether she secures the Republican nomination, Haley's presence in the race is destined to significantly influence the election's dialogue and focus. Her candidacy amplifies crucial issues, compelling other candidates to respond and adapt to her stances. Her emphasis on economic growth, national security, and revitalizing America's global leadership strikes a chord with voters seeking experienced and capable leadership.

Moreover, Haley's campaign possesses the potential to redefine the future trajectory of the Republican Party. As a woman of Indian-

American heritage, she brings diversity and inclusivity to the forefront of the party's agenda. Her candidacy challenges conventional perceptions of a Republican candidate, appealing to a broader voter base and reshaping the party's image.

Chapter 7: Impact of Trump's Legal Issues

Former President Donald Trump's quest for the Republican nomination in the 2024 presidential election is fraught with an array of legal entanglements that continue to command widespread attention. Among the prominent cases shadowing him, the Trump Organization's involvement in a civil fraud suit in New York stands out prominently. The lawsuit alleges manipulations of property values aimed at securing more favorable financing terms. New York's state Attorney General is aggressively pursuing penalties exceeding $250 million and seeking a prohibition on Trump and his sons from managing businesses in New York. This high-stakes trial compounds Trump's already extensive legal challenges.

Beyond the New York civil fraud suit, Trump faces another significant legal battle in Georgia. This case accuses him of orchestrating an extensive effort to overturn his defeat in the 2020 presidential election. Its implications go beyond individual charges, as it questions the sanctity of the democratic process, shedding light on Trump's attempts to contest the election outcome.

Adding to his legal woes, Trump confronts a daunting 34 counts of falsifying business records in Manhattan. These charges stem from hush money payments made to adult film actress Stormy Daniels prior to the 2016 presidential election. Throughout these legal battles, Trump maintains his innocence, pleading not guilty in each criminal case.

The ramifications of these legal issues on Trump's presidential ambitions remain uncertain. Should these criminal and civil cases progress swiftly, Trump might find himself juggling the rigors of the campaign trail while awaiting legal resolutions. The outcomes could potentially impact his eligibility to run for president, as lawsuits in multiple states seek to disqualify him from the presidency. However, despite these legal challenges, Trump remains one of the leading Republican contenders in the race for the presidency.

The resolution of the ongoing legal conflicts surrounding former President Donald Trump carries immense weight, holding the key to his future in politics. These cases go far beyond determining his innocence or guilt; they possess the potential for significant legal ramifications. Their outcomes are poised to deeply influence public perception, thereby impacting the support Trump garners from voters.

As these legal dramas unfold, the nation's attention is riveted on how they will shape Trump's chances of securing the Republican nomination and possibly staging a comeback to the presidency. The repercussions of these battles extend beyond Trump's personal trajectory, reaching into the broader landscape of American politics. Indeed, they have the potential to redefine the contours of political accountability and reshape the prevailing political discourse.

The public's judgment regarding these matters will be instrumental in shaping not only Trump's future but also setting precedents for the conduct and expectations of future political leaders. The weight of these legal challenges extends beyond mere political consequences;

they have the capacity to set a tone for the behavior and actions of aspiring leaders in the future.

Crucially, these legal conflicts are at the epicenter of a pivotal moment that will significantly influence the trajectory of American politics. The nation will keenly observe how these cases unfold, recognizing the potential for far-reaching consequences that transcend Trump's personal political future and extend to the broader political landscape.

Chapter 8: The Third-Party Factor

As of December 2023, the landscape for the 2024 United States presidential election is taking form, notably with the emergence of several influential third-party candidates. Among them, Robert F. Kennedy Jr. stands out prominently. His departure from the Democratic Party primaries and subsequent surge in early polling reflect a considerable level of support for his independent candidacy. Kennedy's decision to run independently underscores a belief in an alternative political approach, resonating strongly with a segment of the electorate yearning for a fresh perspective.

Adding to the intrigue is the potential candidacy of Sen. Joe Manchin III, a West Virginia Democrat who recently announced his decision not to seek re-election and is reportedly leaning towards a presidential run under the No Labels ticket. Manchin's move to distance himself from traditional party lines echoes the sentiments of an electorate increasingly disenchanted with partisan politics, seeking pragmatic solutions to the nation's pressing challenges.

Moreover, other notable individuals have thrown their hats into the ring as independents or prospective nominees of unspecified third parties, including Shiva Ayyadurai, Joseph "Afroman" Foreman, and Taylor Marshall. Their entry into the race injects diversity and unpredictability, offering unique perspectives and ideas that contribute to the dynamic nature of the upcoming election.

It's important to note that the Libertarian Party and various minor parties are also anticipated to nominate their respective candidates, further enriching the diversity of the 2024 presidential ballot. This array of third-party candidates mirrors a growing voter desire for alternatives beyond the two major political parties. Observing how their presence shapes the political discourse and influences the final election outcome promises to be a captivating aspect of this election cycle.

The looming prospect of third-party candidates influencing the 2024 presidential race presents a significant concern, injecting an element of unpredictability that could sway the outcome in unforeseen ways. The emergence of outsider contenders like Robert F. Kennedy Jr. and Cornel West has introduced an air of uncertainty and volatility into the political arena. While these candidates aren't projected to secure the presidency, their presence could divert support away from the major party nominees, potentially reshaping the election results. History has shown that third-party candidates can wield considerable influence, altering the course of past elections.

This phenomenon largely stems from a faction of dissatisfied voters disenchanted with the limitations of the two-party system. These voters seek solace in alternative platforms espoused by these third-party candidates, driven by a desire for options that better mirror their values and convictions. As a consequence, their ascent introduces a layer of unpredictability to the race, posing challenges to established norms and raising questions about the influence they might exert.

The impact of third-party candidates transcends merely attracting voters from major contenders. Their presence significantly contributes to shaping political discourse and influencing policy discussions. By presenting diverse choices and perspectives, they enrich the landscape of a pluralistic democracy. However, their introduction also adds a level of complexity and uncertainty, making it challenging to predict their exact impact on the race and subsequent governance.

Democratic officials, in particular, have voiced apprehensions regarding the potential sway of third-party candidates, recognizing the historical precedent of their role in election outcomes. As the 2024 presidential race approaches, concerns and scrutiny surrounding the role of these candidates continue to mount.

Their potential to disrupt the electoral landscape and potentially alter the trajectory of the election underscores the necessity for a comprehensive understanding of their influence and the implications for the democratic process. Voters are confronted with choices that prompt reflection on the consequences of supporting third-party candidates and their implications for the broader political landscape.

The presence of third-party candidates injecting uncertainty into the electoral landscape introduces a fascinating dimension to the democratic process. It serves as a reminder of the dynamic nature of democracy, emphasizing the importance of active political involvement and the careful evaluation of choices presented to voters.

The potential influence of third-party candidates underscores the vitality of a system that allows for diverse voices and perspectives. Their participation challenges the status quo, compelling voters to engage more deeply in the political discourse. This engagement is crucial, as it encourages citizens to explore a wider range of policy proposals, ideologies, and potential leaders.

Moreover, the emergence of third-party contenders emphasizes the need for voters to make informed and thoughtful decisions. It prompts individuals to critically assess the platforms and values represented by each candidate, fostering a deeper understanding of the broader political landscape.

By presenting alternative choices, third-party candidates inspire voters to consider options beyond the traditional party lines. This expansion of choices elevates the discourse, promoting a more nuanced understanding of the multifaceted issues facing the nation.

Ultimately, the presence of third-party candidates serves as a catalyst for increased civic participation and a call for heightened awareness among voters. It encourages citizens to actively shape the political direction of their country by making informed choices aligned with their beliefs and values. In this way, the specter of third-party candidates complicating the race underscores the essence of democracy: a dynamic system that thrives on diverse perspectives, robust engagement, and thoughtful consideration of the array of options presented to the electorate.

Chapter 9: Media Spotlight and Public Engagement

The forthcoming 2024 presidential election is poised to command substantial media attention, drawing the gaze of audiences not just within the United States but also globally. Extensive coverage and in-depth analysis of the candidates, their policies, and the campaign dynamics will be pivotal in informing the public and shaping discussions surrounding this consequential event. The significance of this election is immense, as its outcome will determine the trajectory of the nation for the next four years and potentially influence a spectrum of policy issues.

However, amidst this media spotlight, the evolving media landscape presents unique challenges for the upcoming election. Among the most pressing concerns is the emergence of "deep fakes" — manipulated or counterfeit videos capable of misleading viewers by presenting false information. These deceptive deep fakes not only have the potential to misinform the public but also cast doubt on the credibility of legitimate news sources. Navigating this new terrain will demand meticulous verification of content by journalists and media entities to counter the spread of misinformation.

Additionally, a notable challenge the media will confront is the diminishing trust in traditional news sources. In recent times, there has been a growing skepticism towards established media outlets, with many questioning their objectivity and accuracy. Rebuilding this trust is imperative for journalists striving to deliver accurate and impartial reporting during the election season. Media organizations must endeavor to restore confidence among their audience by emphasizing transparency and accountability in their reporting practices.

Moreover, the potential involvement of former President Donald Trump in the 2024 election introduces an unprecedented element to the media landscape. Trump's prior presidency was marked by his unorthodox communication style and extensive use of social media platforms to directly engage with the public. Should he decide to run again, his campaign is anticipated to be influential and intensely scrutinized by the media. This could reshape conventional dynamics of political campaigning and media coverage, given Trump's unique ability to captivate and polarize public opinion.

Nevertheless, despite these challenges, the comprehensive media coverage and analysis surrounding the 2024 election will equip voters with a wealth of information. This heightened engagement will empower individuals to make informed decisions when casting their ballots, as they will access a broad spectrum of perspectives and policy proposals. The media's role as a watchdog and a platform for political discourse will foster dynamic discussions on pivotal issues and hold candidates accountable for their actions and statements.

It's crucial to acknowledge that the evolving media landscape, coupled with the potential influence of emerging technologies and political developments, will shape the narrative and coverage of the 2024 election in distinctive ways. The interaction between traditional news outlets and social media platforms will continue to significantly impact information dissemination and public opinion.

Adaptation to these changes will be vital for media organizations, necessitating the embrace of new technologies and innovative approaches to effectively engage with their audience.

In essence, the upcoming 2024 presidential election is poised to captivate global attention, serving as a significant focal point across media platforms worldwide. Amidst challenges like the proliferation of deep fakes and a waning trust in traditional news sources, journalists and media outlets are poised to offer expansive coverage and detailed analysis, empowering voters with essential information and fostering a vibrant and engaging election season.

The evolving media landscape, marked by technological advancements and the omnipresence of social media, shapes a unique terrain for this electoral cycle. This dynamic interplay of traditional journalism and digital platforms is poised to redefine the dissemination of information and public perception, adding an unprecedented layer of complexity to the election's narrative and coverage.

The potential reentry of former President Donald Trump into the political arena significantly amplifies the intrigue surrounding this election. Trump's unconventional approach to communication and his substantial influence on public opinion through social media during his presidency indicate that his participation, if materialized, could fundamentally impact the dynamics of political campaigning and media coverage.

However, despite these challenges and potential disruptions, the comprehensive coverage and insightful analysis provided by journalists and media entities promise to equip voters with the necessary tools to make informed decisions. This collective effort contributes to an election environment characterized by depth, dynamism, and informed engagement, allowing citizens to weigh diverse perspectives and policy proposals before casting their votes.

Chapter 10: Breaking Down the Timeline

The path to Election Day 2024 is paved with crucial milestones. The primaries and caucuses, starting in January, will shape the field and offer insights into voter preferences. Super Tuesday, with numerous states holding primaries, and the national conventions in July and August will further refine the race and solidify candidates.

The 2024 presidential election is marked by several crucial milestones that will shape the political landscape. The primaries and caucuses, commencing in January, will play a pivotal role in delineating the field of candidates and providing insights into voter preferences[2]. Super Tuesday, scheduled for March 5, will further refine the race, with over a dozen states, including California and Texas, holding their primaries[2]. The national conventions in July and August will serve to solidify the candidates for the general election[2]. However, the potential influence of third-party and independent candidates, such as Robert F. Kennedy Jr. and Cornel West, has introduced an element of uncertainty, as their presence could siphon votes away from the major contenders, potentially impacting the outcome in unexpected ways[4][5]. This dynamic political landscape underscores the significance of the upcoming election and the potential for unforeseen developments to shape its trajectory.

The 2024 US presidential election is shaping up to be a fascinating and critical event in American politics. To navigate this complex journey, it's essential to understand the timeline and the key phases involved. The first phase is the Primaries and Caucuses, which typically take place from January to June.

During this period, candidates engage in fierce battles to secure their party's nomination by earning delegates in each state. Some crucial events to watch out for during this phase include the Iowa Caucuses, held on February 4th, which traditionally set the tone for the rest of the race. Super Tuesday, on March 12th, sees 14 states hold primaries, including influential states like California and Texas. Another notable event is the New Hampshire Primary, taking place on March 19th, renowned for its engaged voters and early impact on the election. Additionally, each state has its own schedule and rules for primaries and caucuses, contributing to the delegate count throughout this phase.

Once the primaries and caucuses are complete, the second phase kicks in: the National Conventions. These grandiose events, held in July and August, are where the parties gather their delegates and formally select their candidates. The Republican National Convention, taking place from July 15th to 18th in Milwaukee, Wisconsin, is where Republicans solidify their platform and unveil their nominee. Similarly, the Democratic National Convention, held from August 19th to 22nd in Chicago, Illinois, is where Democrats showcase their candidate and present their vision for the future.

Following the National Conventions, the third phase commences: the General Election Campaign. This period, spanning from September to November, is characterized by intense competition between the two nominees as they engage in debates, rallies, and media appearances to win the votes of the American people. Three official presidential debates are scheduled, hosted by the Commission on Presidential Debates, providing a platform for the candidates to discuss key issues and highlight their contrasting visions. Both candidates also crisscross the nation, holding rallies and town halls, where they directly meet voters and energize their respective bases. Additionally, many states offer early voting options, allowing citizens to cast their ballots before Election Day.

Finally, the fourth phase consists of the Post-Election Activities, taking place from November to January. The pinnacle of this phase is Election Day, which falls on November 5th. On this day, Americans head to the polls to cast their votes and determine the next president and vice president. Subsequently, in December, the Electoral College convenes to officially cast their votes, ultimately deciding the winner. This step is crucial as it solidifies the election results.

Finally, on January 20th, Inauguration Day arrives, marking the official swearing-in of the newly elected president and vice president and signaling the beginning of a new term.

It is important to note that this timeline is a general overview, and specific dates may vary depending on state regulations and party rules. It is vital to stay informed and follow updates as the election draws closer to ensure an accurate understanding of the process. The 2024 US presidential election promises to be a captivating journey, and being well-informed about the timeline will enable individuals to navigate its twists and turns effectively.

So, in summary:

Phase 1: Primaries and Caucuses (January - June): This phase determines the nominees of each party, with key events like Super Tuesday and the Iowa caucuses.

Phase 2: National Conventions (July - August): The parties formally choose their candidates and solidify their platforms at these conventions.

Phase 3: General Election Campaign (September - November): The race heats up with debates, rallies, and early voting. Election Day on November 5th determines the winner.

Phase 4: Post-Election Activities (November - January): The Electoral College meets in December, and Inauguration Day on January 20th marks the official start of the new presidential term.

So again, and to make clear:

The American presidential election process unfolds in four distinct phases, extending over several months and embodying the essence of democracy in action.

Phase one, spanning from January to June, kicks off with the primaries and caucuses. Here, candidates within each political party vie for their party's nomination. Critical events like Super Tuesday and the Iowa caucuses set the tone, often serving as pivotal moments shaping the race and identifying front-runners.

Phase two, known as the National Conventions, spans from July to August. During this period, the parties officially nominate their candidates and solidify their platforms. These highly anticipated conventions convene party members, delegates, and political luminaries nationwide. It's here that candidates formally accept their party's nomination and outline their vision for the country.

The third phase, the General Election Campaign, spans from September to November and constitutes the most intense and critical stage. Candidates engage in a rigorous campaign, participating in debates, organizing rallies, and mobilizing their supporters. The competition intensifies as candidates aim to sway undecided voters and secure electoral votes. Concurrently, early voting occurs, allowing citizens to cast ballots before the designated Election Day.

Election Day itself falls on November 5th, culminating the General Election Campaign. On this pivotal day, American citizens head to the polls to cast their votes, ultimately determining the presidential election's victor.

The candidate securing the majority of electoral votes becomes the President-elect.

The fourth and final phase, Post-Election Activities, spans from November to January. During this period, the Electoral College convenes in December to officially cast their votes, solidifying the election results. Then, on January 20th—Inauguration Day—the newly elected President is sworn into office, marking the commencement of their term.

In essence, the American presidential election process comprises these four integral phases: Primaries and Caucuses, National Conventions, General Election Campaign, and Post-Election Activities. Each phase contributes significantly to shaping the election's course, from nominating party candidates to officially inaugurating the President. This structured process stands as a testament to the democratic principles upon which the United States was founded, emphasizing public participation and the power of the vote in determining the nation's leadership.

Chapter 11: Observing the Race

Prepare yourself for the upcoming presidential election journey by following this comprehensive guide. First and foremost, staying informed is paramount. Seek out reliable news sources that present diverse perspectives and rigorously fact-check their reporting. Avoid falling into echo chambers or being swayed by partisan spin, which can distort your understanding of the candidates and their policies. Dive deeper into articles, attend town halls, and watch unbiased debates to truly grasp each candidate's positions. Engage in a fact-finding mission by questioning everything, verifying claims, and challenging your own biases. Informed decisions necessitate critical thinking.

Another crucial aspect is active involvement in the democratic process. Consider volunteering for a campaign—whether it's canvassing, phone banking, or data entry, your time and effort significantly contribute to democratic success. Ensure you're registered to vote and encourage others to do the same. Your voice holds weight, and it's vital to ensure it's heard on Election Day. Organizing or participating in local events like debates, watch parties, or community discussions can foster vibrant discourse and draw others into the political conversation.

Respecting diverse perspectives is foundational for a robust democracy. Actively listen to differing viewpoints, even when they conflict with your own beliefs. Understanding the rationale behind different ideologies can broaden your perspectives. Engage in respectful dialogue, prioritize open communication, and avoid personal attacks. Strive to find common ground, acknowledging that we're all part of this collective journey. Celebrate the variety of voices and embrace the depth of debate, even amidst disagreements.

When it comes to the election itself, concentrate on the issues that hold significance for you and your community. Cut through the noise and personalities that often dominate the political sphere. Refrain from getting swept up in drama or sensationalized reports that detract from the real issues at hand. Take time to analyze the candidates' policies and delve into their stances on critical topics like healthcare, education, and the economy. Understand how their plans will impact your life and those around you. Hold the candidates accountable by posing questions at town halls, writing letters to your representatives, and ensuring your voice is heard. Always remember, they work for you.

The upcoming 2024 election presents an extraordinary opportunity for individuals like you to not only engage but truly shape the course of your country's future. It stands as a powerful platform for you to express your beliefs, stay well-informed, and actively contribute to the transformative change you envision for your nation. To make a meaningful impact during this momentous period, it's vital to remain informed about the candidates, their policies, and the critical issues facing the nation.

Active participation in political discourse can be accomplished by engaging in discussions, attending town halls, and seeking information from reliable and credible sources. This proactive approach equips you with the necessary tools to navigate the fascinating journey of a presidential election effectively.

Approaching these conversations with an open mind and respect for diverse perspectives is equally crucial. Engaging respectfully with individuals who hold differing viewpoints can broaden your understanding, allowing you to cultivate a more nuanced and well-rounded opinion.

Focusing on the issues that matter most to you and your community serves as a guiding principle in making a tangible impact. Whether your concerns lie in areas like climate change, education, healthcare, social justice, or other pressing matters, identifying these crucial topics empowers you to channel your energy and efforts towards advocating for meaningful change in these specific areas.

Consider this guide as your compass, offering guidance and encouragement to actively participate in political discourse. Your engagement in the democratic process holds the potential to shape the trajectory of your country's future and leave a lasting impact on generations to come.

Embrace this opportunity with confidence, knowing that your voice carries significance and can contribute to shaping a more just and prosperous future for your nation. Let your voice reverberate in the chorus of change, and play your part in the collective journey towards progress and a better tomorrow.

Chapter 12: Staying Informed and Engaged

The 2024 presidential election is an upcoming event that holds immense importance. It brings with it a flood of information, opinions, and passionate debates that can sometimes leave individuals feeling overwhelmed or lost. However, fear not, for staying informed and engaged is your superpower in this critical election. It is the key to making well-informed decisions, contributing to a vibrant democratic process, and ultimately shaping the future of your nation.

To step into your full power, it is crucial to become a News Ninja. Seek out reliable sources that offer a diverse range of perspectives, ditching the echo chambers and partisan spin. Don't stop at the headlines; dive deeper into articles, watch unbiased debates, and attend town halls to understand the nuances of each candidate's position. Remember to verify, verify, verify. Don't take everything at face value. Question claims, research statistics, and maintain a healthy skepticism towards sensationalized reports.

Engaging beyond the screen is equally important. Attend candidate events, town halls, and local debates to step into the real world. Hear the candidates firsthand, ask questions, and observe their interactions with voters. Engage in respectful conversations with people who hold different views, actively listening, seeking common ground, and avoiding personal attacks. It is crucial to remember that we are all in this together. By volunteering for a campaign, registering voters in your community, or organizing discussions and events, you can join the movement and make a meaningful impact.

It is essential to focus on the issues, not the noise. Cut through the drama and personalities that often dominate election cycles. Instead, channel your energy towards the issues that matter to you and your community. Analyze the candidates' policies, researching their stances on healthcare, education, the economy, and other crucial topics. Understand how their plans will impact your life and the nation as a whole. Hold them accountable by asking questions at events, writing letters to your representatives, and making your voice heard. Remember, they work for you.

By staying informed, engaging in respectful discourse, and prioritizing the issues that matter, you become an active participant in the democratic process. You are not just a spectator; you are a voice, a force for change, and a vital part of shaping the future of your nation. So, citizen, take up your news sword, attend the town hall battles, and raise your voice in respectful debate. The 2024 election is your chance to be heard, to be informed, and to be the change you want to see. Remember, your power lies in your information, your engagement, and your focus. Use it wisely, and make this election journey your own.

Dr. David K. Ewen

The 2024 Showdown

Inside the Race for the White House

By

Dr. David K. Ewen